Dolores Wycoff began writing as a teenager and though she taught for over 50 years, her passion has always been writing. She wrote children's picture books to illustrate learning points in the classroom. She has written and received awards for her poetry. She spoke in Edinburgh at the Conference of Arts and Communication. Even though she is losing her eyesight – she continues with her passion.

Dedicated to those who have been on the journey of faith
and have found peace and hope for their hearts and spirits.

Dolores Wyckoff

# PSALMS: A JOURNEY OF FAITH

AUSTIN MACAULEY PUBLISHERS™
LONDON • CAMBRIDGE • NEW YORK • SHARJAH

**Ordering Information**
Quantity sales: Special discounts are available on quantity purchases by corporations, associations, and others. For details, contact the publisher at the address below.

**Publisher's Cataloging-in-Publication data**
Wyckoff, Dolores
Psalms: A Journey of Faith

ISBN 9798891551848 (Paperback)
ISBN 9798891551855 (ePub e-book)

Library of Congress Control Number: 2024908832

www.austinmacauley.com/us

First Published 2024
Austin Macauley Publishers LLC
40 Wall Street, 33rd Floor, Suite 3302
New York, NY 10005
USA

mail-usa@austinmacauley.com
+1 (646) 5125767

# Foreword

Some years ago, I was going through a diffcult time and the best help and encouragement I could get was from the book of Psalms. As I read, I thought these are
David's words. I began to put the scriptures into my words from my heart as I cried out to God. And thus, this book *Psalms: A Journey of Faith* was born. It is my prayer that as you read it, you will share your own words from your heart to a loving and compassionate God. I will be praying for you.

Dolores

# Psalm 1:3

By cool flowing streams
God has planted me,
Living water pouring from God's throne.
I am a tree, full of life, yielding fruit.
Oh yes, I will bear fruit.
I will expose myself to that stream,
Drawing strength and nourishment,
Reaching out my arms
To those who are weary
And hungry for food to feed the soul.
Come and sit under my branches,
Eat the fruit God has provided.
I will not wither or fall into decay.
My roots are firmly planted.
I will not waver or be blown
About by every wind and scheme.
I am a tree planted by God.

# Psalm 3

Lord I am bound on all sides.
They laugh at me and mock me.
"O ho" they say, "Your god won't help you."
But I know better.
When I cry to You, You are quick to hear me.
You give me strength.
You are my place of rest.
Why am I so fearful?
I walk in the assurance of Your salvation.

# Psalm 3:4,6-9

Your name rises, oh Lord
Full of majesty and great power.
Your creation sings out your name.
Glory is Your crown.
Your fingers span the heavens,
Setting the moon and stars in their place.
Yet, You have not forgotten me.
You have made me share Your good works.
There is nothing in heaven or earth
That You have not created.
You reign with great majesty.
Your name is awesome.

# Psalm 5:1,2,3,7,8,11

Oh LORD, are you listening?
Do You hear me cry?
I soak my pillow with my tears each night.
Morning brings me fresh hope.
Once again I come to You.
Your throne room is open to me.
And I can look up into Your face.
I remember Who it is that guides my steps.
My tears are turned to shouts of joy.
Yes, yes You do hear me.
Because I am trusting you.

# Psalm 9:1,2,9,10

My heart is an open book before You, Lord.
I will testify of Your goodness toward me,
Holding nothing back.
Excitement runs through me,
I cannot be silent, I must sing.
Even my enemy cannot stop me
From praising Your Name.
What can they do to me?
I run safely to You and hide.
I know You and trust You.
Your arms are always open to me.

# Psalm 13

Where are You, oh Lord?
I cannot find You.
I know you are there.
My enemy is laughing at me.
I am sad because You do not answer me.
Of course You are there, Lord.
You've always been there.
Your love is unending.
My heart cannot keep from rejoicing.
I will sing of Your eternal goodness.

# Psalm 16:1,2,3

From the depths of my heart
I say to you Lord,
I trust You and am nothing without You.
You giver me purpose.
You hold me steady
You instructions are the reins of my life.
You have chosen my way.
I am pleased to walk that path.
It brings me joy that will never end.

# Psalm 17:1,4,8,15

I open before You Lord.
I have no need to hide.
By Your Word I have avoided,
The snares of my soul's enemy.
Set my feet on a solid path
Then I will not slip.
I am safely hidden,
But You do not hide Yourself from me.
You hear the words my heart speaks.

# Psalm 18:3,30,33,35

Oh Lord, You are a strong rock,
A place of safety.
I will not fall when I stand on your Word.
It is my firm foundation.
I lay hold of my salvation,
I am strengthened.
You will direct my paths.
You will give me hind feet
So I can stand in high places.
You have placed weapons in my hands.
I will defeat my enemy.
You are my shield and victory.
In your gentleness, I am strong.
I can walk confidently on a safe path

# Psalm 19:7-11, 14

There is nothing as perfect as Your Word.

I can trust in it.
Your Word gives me joy
And your truth brings light to my soul.
It shines out of me,
There is nothing hidden.
Your laws are plain to see,
They taste good and I am satisfied.
Gold cannot buy them
Nor can honey bring such sweetness to my life.
You instruct me and guide me.
I find great peace when I listen to You
Take delight in my prayers and praise.
I acknowledge Your greatness and Your strength.

# Psalm 20:3,4,7,8

As my prayers go up to you.
I am coincident that you will hear me.
You are not a god without ears.
You will honor your Word.
I can depend on your faithfulness.
Your Name is the banner over me.
I can stand tall in times of trouble.
My King has won the victory.

# Psalm 23

You have become my Shepherd.
I do not lack anything.
A green pasture is my resting place,
Peaceful streams refresh me.
You will guide me down the right path
Because I am Yours.
Even when the path goes through a dark place
And I feel my life is being drawn away,
There is no fear in me
Because You are here.
You protect me from danger,
And sometimes You carry me.
You show me Your care in front of my enemies.
You have chosen me, and I am overjoyed.
I will always be surrounded by Your love.
You are my eternal dwelling place.

# Psalm 24:1,7,8

The earth belongs to the Lord,
As does everything that inhabits the earth.
Not only the earth
But the seas and skies, also
And all who dwell therein-
Raise up your head, your gates
And be raised up you aged portals.
Welcome the One who is great in majesty
Who is the royal personage?
It is the Lord full of might and power.
Victorious in battle is the Lord!

# Psalm 25:1-6

I lay bare my soul to You, Lord
Because I know I can trust You.
Do not let me hang my head in shame
Or give my enemies a reason to gloat.
If I trust in You,
Then You will give me confidence.
Shame will come to those
Whose purpose is against You.
Open my eyes, Lord
And guide my feet to walk Your way.
You are my God who saves me.
Everyday You are my source of hope.
From the beginning
Your love and mercy have been a part of You.

# Psalm 26:1,2,3,7,9,11,12

Stand for me LORD
Speak for me.
I have measured my steps,
I have walked the path of truth.
What can I say?
I will tell of your goodness,
Of Your never-failing love for me
It has been sweet to sit under.
Your glory To taste of Your mercy.
I will not forget to praise you.

# Psalm 28:1,2,6,7

I call to You, Lord, because You are my anchor.
Please listen to me.
If You do not answer me
Then I will be as those who fall away from You.
I am pleading for mercy.
Your are the only one who can help me.
I reach toward Your throne, Your mercy seat
I sing praises to the Lord.
You have heard my pitiful cry,
And You pour Your strength into me
And are my shield of protection.
In my heart, I know You can be trusted
As a lamb trusts its shepherd in the field
And that gives me peace.
Because I am full of joy
My song is one of thanks to You, oh my God.

# Psalm 29:1,2,3,4,10

All who are powerful
Must acknowledge You, Lord.
What are they compared to You?
You deserve our worship,
You, only, are worthy to be worshiped.
Your holiness is brilliant and awesome.
You command the universe
And all creation just by speaking.
You speak in authority with a loud voice.
Everything moves beneath Your throne.
There is no end to You
Your are king!
You give me strength because I am Yours.
I am surrounded by Your blessings
And walk in peace.

# Psalm 30:2,3,4,5,12

I hurt so bad LORD.
Sometimes I ache because of the torment.
Of those around me.
But You bring healing to my heart and soul.
You open the door of my prison
And set me free.
You promise me joy.
That the morning will come.
I feel a song bursting out of me.
It can't be silent.
You deserve my song of praise.

# Psalms 33:1-3,6,18,20

I will sing with my heart to You, oh Lord.

I must praise You,

That is why I am here,

Even though the harp and the lyre

Are instruments of praise,

I have my own song to sing to You.

It is a song of joy.

You breathed out the stars without a number.

You gave the seas boundaries

And yet You have chosen me for an inheritance.

Your eyes are upon me.

Because I know You,

I rest in Your love.

# Psalm 34:1-4

I will never stop praising You, Lord.
Words of adoration will
Always comes from my lips.
My very heart is in tune with You
And declares that You are my God.
Anyone who is in pain will hear me
And will also be joyful.
Together,we will lift up Your Name.
You hear me when I call
And calm my fears... all of them.

# Psalm 37:1-7

I must not worry so when evil men prosper.
Nothing they have will last.
If I hide myself in You, then I am safe.
You want me to be soft and pliable,
To share my heart with You.
If I trust You completely
Then others will see Your light in me.
If I am patient and stand still,
I will see Your hand at work.
I know You are in control,
Lord, why is it that wicked men
Seem to prosper?
You have promised to break their power.
The faithful will be lifted up.

# Psalm 40:1-4.17

I sat quietly waiting for You, Lord.

When I cried, You were there to comfort me.

When I slipped and fell,

And the ground under my feet was shaky

You lifted me up

And gave me a safe place to stand.

I could sing my own song.

I could love You with my song.

Come and see that He is a God you can trust,.

Even though I have nothing, I am rich.

You are always there for me.

# Psalm 42:1-5, 8

Just as the deer searches out the clear streams,
So I seek the living water that comes from God.
Then my thirst is quenched.
How long must I wait?
Show me where You are
That I might run to You.
I have known the anticipation and joy
That comes from praising God.
My nights are full of weeping,
My days have no relief from my tears.
I remember how it used to be.
"Wait…don't be sad," I say to my soul.
I can still sing to my God.
I can feel Your love during the day.
I can hear You at night.
Your song is within my heart.
I pour my heart out to You.

# Psalm 46:1-7, 10

God, You are my hiding place.
You are always nearby.
I can reach out and touch You.
Fear will not overwhelm me.
Even if the mountains move around
And the sea boils and chums,
There is a place where God dwells.
It is eternal and cannot be changed.
Governments are rising and falling.
The earth is being broken apart,
But I am safe in Your protection.
You want me to be quiet
And know that You are the I AM.

# Psalm 51:1-4, 7-10

I don't deserve the that comes to me
Because of Your great love.
It is because of Your intense compassion
That you have covered my sins.
Your forgiveness washes over me
Making me clean.
I can't seem to forget my sin.
It haunts me.
My sin brings You pain.
It deserves Your judgment.
Put a brand new heart in me
And give me a spirit of faithfulness.

# Psalm 54:1-7

There is salvation in Your Name, oh God.

You are strong enough to save me.

Open Your ears to my cry for help.

I am surrounded by terror

And my life is in danger.

They do not know my God.

My God has not deserted me.

You will bless those who reach out to me.

You will punish those who seek to hurt me.

Your truth will win.

My enemies flee when I cry to Your for help.

You are always there for me.

I will extol your Word.

I will continue to trust in You.

# Psalm 56:3,4; 8-11

I know that you are there
When I am afraid.
Your Word is trustworthy.
I can depend on You.
I don't need to be afraid.
Nothing can hurt me
Because you know where I am.
You take note of my tears and
Treasure them in Your bottle.
I will praise You openly.
Your Name is good and deserves to be praised.

# Psalm 59:4, 8, 8m, 16-17

Lord, I am surrounded
By those who would do harm to me.
No matter where I turn
I am oppressed by those
Who does not have good intentions toward me.
But you will show them I am not alone and weak.
You will be my shield and defender.
You are made strong in my weakness.
I will not forget to praise You.
I will sing loudly.
I will declare that You, alone, are my defense,
My merciful God.

# Psalm 61:1-4, 8

Where are You, Lord?
I run everywhere, crying out to You.
My heart is breaking
And I will drown in my tears.
Help me to find a rock to stand on.
I must remember that You have
Always been a place of safety for me;
A tower the enemy could not reach.
I will stay in that safe place.
I will crawl under Your wings
Like a baby chick.
I will not forget to praise You.
I will keep my promises to You.

# Psalm 62:1, 2, 5-8

I wait quietly for you, God.
I am not depending on my own strength.
I know I cannot be shaken.
You are my line of defense,
I won't be driven back.
I can hope with confidence
Because You are my confidence
And my surety.
I am vulnerable because of you.
You accept me as I am
And still hold me close,
Pushing away all danger.

# Psalm 63:4,5,6,7,7

Oh God, you are real to me
I will meet with You early in the morning.
When every day seems dry and tasteless
You are able to refresh me.
I have searched for You.
Nothing compares to the kindness You show me.
When I lift up my hands and praise you,
Then I know what it means to be satisfied.
In the night darkness
Help me to remember the light
When you were with me.
When morning comes,
You are still there

# Psalm 66:1-12

I am so free!

I can shout Your Name.

All around me, I see the works of Your hand.

Your are awesome!

Everyone who opposes You

Will know You are God.

Even the earth sings Your praises,

I can't be quiet.

You help me stand firm.

I am going through the refiner's fire

And I will come out as pure silver.

You always go through the fire with me.

Now I can make an offering to you,

One that is sweet and fragrant.

# Psalm 71:1-8

When I turn to You, Lord
You help me to hold my head up.
You listen to me.
No matter how often I run to You
There is always a place for me.
From my conception
You have held me.
Thank You for always being there for me.
Everything in me acknowledges who You are.
Don't forsake me now.
I need you more than ever.
I will sing of your holiness.
I will be an instrument of praise.

# Psalm 73

I am troubled Lord.
The wicked laugh and are carefree.
They flaunt Your laws.
I am an alien in their world.
Now I understand.
Judgment will come.
And darkness will be brought to light.
Then I will remember,
You are my strength and my joy.
I would not trade my life in You.
For such a fleeting moment of pleasure here.

# Pslam 77

I cried out loud to my God.
You turned Your ear toward my call.
You, who have done such awesome things.
Everything in maturer hears and obeys You.
How can I so easily forget?
Bring Your works and promises to my remembrances.
You are the same
You don't change.

# Psalm 84

Lord I long for the day
When I can stand in
You presence.
Your house will be full of praise.
I will bass my voice to the song.
No darkness only the light of Your Presence.
Peace will settle in like a blanket.
No fear, only trust.

# Psalm 91:1-6

As long as I make You my abiding place,
I am safe.
You are the strong fortress I can run into.
Sometimes I feel trapped.
With now way out.
You will open the trap and set me free.
When shadows hover over me at night,
You bring light into the darkness.
It is as bright as day.
I am not afraid anymore.

# Psalm 92

I came into Your sanctuary
With a song on my lips,
My song blends with that of others praisers
We are in harmony
I too. Am the work of Your hands,
I am planted in Your court.
I have a purpose,
I declare to everyone who listens
How blessed I am

# Psalm 95

I sing. I can shout
I can bow down.
I can become an instrument of praise.
I am in harmony
With all creation.
Together we worship
The God who made us

# Psalm 69:1.11,12

You have given me a new song to sing.
I give praise to You.
V iv song ions the song of creation.
Listen from earth to heaven,
I hear happy music.
The sea roars out of tune,
Even the fields and trees join with joy

# Psalm 98:1,4-8

It is hard to be still when
I see everything God is doing
I just want to burst into song
How can I help it?
I can join with all creation,
The earth and seas, rivers and hills
Heavenly music is our accompaniment

# Psalm 102

No one listens to me but You Lord.
Don't close Your ears to my prayer.
I feel so alone and lost.
Is there no one who
Will reach out to take my hand.
They look at me blankly.
Shaking their heads and curling their lips.
I have no one but you, Lord

# Psalm 103:1-5

I am filled with love for You, Lord.
Every fiber of my body praises you,
You have made me free and whole again.
I am clean in Your eyes,
You clothed me in love and tenderness
You have given me the strength to go on.

# Psalm 104

Oh my God, how great You are.
So majestic: so awesome
There is light all around you I see
You everywhere I turn,
The wind and clouds do Your bidding.
The very earth was laid by You.
All creation obeys You.
The plants and animals depend on Your provision
Everything in all the universe
Moves in harmony with Your will.
And yet. You are mindful of me
As I add my praise and my song

# Psalm 105:1-5

I must remember it is the Lord I seek
It is the Lord I praise and worship.
I want everyone to know Him.
I seek His face and don't look back.
Ahead of me are all the promises He made.
And He will keep them. He never changes.
He still does awesome work.

# Psalm 106:1-5

I can give thanks because He is good
And His mercy on me.
I can't do what He does,
But I can praise Him
In my small way.
When You think about Your chosen,
Remember me.
Don't forget me.
Show me Your favor, also
So that I can glorify You.

# Psalm 113:1-3

I am so blessed to be called His servant
How can I not return the blessings back to Him?
Far as long as I am on this earth,
And then, forever I will continue to praise Him.
Every day, all day, everything I do will praise Him.
I will be a song of praise to him
And call out His name

# Psalm 115:A14,12,13

Lord we cannot claim any glory.
It all belongs to You.
It is because of who You are.
It is because of Your character.
Do their gods have mercy?
Do their gods speak the truth?
No, they do not have mouths to speak,
They are like the ones who made them,
But our God shows His love.
Mercy and great love to us.

# Psalm 119:1-4,10,12,18

You said you bless me,
If I am undefined and walk in Your ways.
But I must also turn my eyes on You
And seek You with my whole heart.
I promise I will keep your commandments.
Only please do not me, alone
I want to learn from You.
So that I can obey You
And please You in everything I do.
And always I will not forget
That You are the Blesser

# Psalm 119:19-32

Every day, as I think about your Words
I am amazed the one so great as You
Would be ready to teach me, guide me
And help me understand Your ways.
I am anxious to learn how I can please You more.
I want You to be pleased with me.
As I run the path You have chosen
My heart sings and is so full of love

# Psalm 11-:33-44,49-50

Teach me your ways,
And give me understanding.
Without this, I cannot
keep your commandments.
With my whole heart
I want to obey you.
I get excited when I hear your voice.
Then I know you're not far off.
Even when I am enticed
By other words, I will not follow them.
When trouble comes,
I remember everything
You told me,
This helps me to stay firm

# Psalm 139:1-6

Lord, You see me exactly as I am.

You know when I am so far down

And when I am swinging high.

You are aware of every thought I have.

Everyday, You know the direction I am going to take.

You are there when I am weary.

I can't hide anything from You.

Every word out of my mouth

Has already passed by you.

You have made a sheltered place for me.

You are my covering.

I don't understand any of this.

My mind cannot grasp Your love.

# Psalms139:13-18

You made me who I am.
I was sheltered by You
In the quietness of the womb.
What can I say?
You carefully shaped me.
You made me something special.
All of Your works are masterpieces.
I am aware of this.
I was in that special place in Your mind.
You made me whole and complete.
You wrote down every aspect of my life
Before it became a reality.
I am still on Your mind,
You have never forgotten me.

# Psalm 141:1,2,4

Lord, I'm begging You.
Please, I need to know
That you are right here with me.
Are You too busy to hear me?
Accept my prayer.
Let the fragrance of my words
Be sweet to you.
By lifting up my hands,
I am giving myself to You.
Protect me from any inclination to do wrong.
Close my ears to the words of ungodly men.
I will not be a part of what they do.
I have made my choice.
I choose You.

# Psalm 142:1-7

I tell you everything
That is in my heart.
I don't hold back anything.
When I feel over-burdened,
I can tell you.
You know where I am.
You see the path I have chosen.
I feel isolated from any help.
No one seems to care.
This is not true.
You are always there.
Please pay attention to me.
Show me the way to freedom.
As I praise You,
Others will join with me.
I am so blessed!

# Psalm143:1-6

Are You listening to me, God?

Can You hear me?

You are the God who never changes.

Everything You do is right.

Do not look at me harshly.

Because I am weak

I don't measure up

To what You consider right.

Everywhere I turn,

I come against something.

I feel trapped and beaten down.

My lie is gone.

There is no life or breath.

I remember when I felt Your presence.

Now I am reaching out.

1 need You, Lord.

# Psalm 144:1,3,19,15

My God is firm and sure.
You teach me how to defend myself.
You are both tender and strong.
You are a place for me to hide
While you stand guard over me.
With music and song I will tell about You.
I will tell how You saved me
Even though I am small and weak
And my life will pass away into a vapor.
It makes me happy to know
That You are my God.

# Psalm 145:1-3, 5-7

My voice will ring with praise of You.
Your name is forever on my tongue.
I will begin each day singing Your praises.
I can not imagine Your majesty.
It is too great.
It is beyond my understanding.
In my thoughts I will concentrate on You,
And then I will speak out
What my heart knows to be true.
Whenever men are declaring
The mighty things You have done,
I will be among them.
My song shall also be heard.

# Psalm 146:1,2, 5-7

From the depths of my being I will praise You.

While I have breath to sing,

I will lift up my voice in praise.

I know You will help me.

I have no one else to run to.

You cannot lie.

You have set the heaven and earth

And sea in their places.

When I am pushed down

You will plead my cause.

I will lack nothing.

I will taste freedom.

You are God,

There is no end to Your reign.

You are forever to be praised.

# Psalm 147:1-3, 5, 6, 11

I am happy when I praise God.
There is a sweetness all around me.
When I feel I am alone,
You hold me.
When my heart is broken,
You wrap me up in Your love.
You understand my feelings
Even when I can't express them.
I can depend on You.
You are strong and will never drop me.

# Psalm 148

I must praise the Lord.
All creation joins me,
We are an instrument of praise.
There is no name equal to Yours.
Your glory is a canopy over me.
You have made the way of salvation for me.
I can hold on to the horns of Your altar.
I will exalt the Lord.

# Psalm 49

I have a new song to sing to the Lord.
I will join with others.
We will praise the Lord together.
You are pleased when we praise You.
The enemy is put to flight.
He has no power, no authority.
When I praise the Lord,
God dwells in my praises.

# Psalm 150

All praise belongs to God.
You are the quiet place.
I will praise You.
Your are in the farthest corners.
I will praise You.
You have done such wonderful and great things.
I will praise You.
Every instrument sings Your praises.
All living creation gives You praise.
I will praise You.